21

JUPITER

Also by Elaine Landau

ELAINE LANDAU

JUPITER

A FIRST BOOK
FRANKLIN WATTS
NEW YORK/LONDON/TORONTO/SYDNEY/1991

For Bari Braunstein

Cover photograph courtesy of: NASA

All photographs courtesy of NASA except: Historical Picture
Service, Chicago: p. 30.

Library of Congress Cataloging-in-Publication Data

Landau, Elaine.
    Jupiter / by Elaine Landau.
        p. cm. — (A First book)
    Includes bibliographical references and index
    Summary: Uses photographs and other recent findings to describe
the atmosphere and geographic features of Jupiter.
        ISBN 0-531-20015-9 (lib. bdg.)—ISBN 0-531-15768-7 (pbk.)
        1. Jupiter (Planet)—Juvenile literature. [1. Jupiter (Planet)]
I. Title. II. Series.
QB661.L36   1991
523.4'5—dc20   90-13099   CIP AC

CONTENTS

24

JUPITER

THE GIANT PLANET

CHAPTER ONE

Jupiter has sometimes been referred to as the giant *planet*. *Astronomers* of ancient times named the shining heavenly body after the Roman king of the gods and ruler of the universe. Jupiter was also called Jove. He was believed to be as powerful as the ancient Greek god Zeus. The ancient symbol for the planet Jupiter is a lightning bolt. It represents the size and strength of the mighty god after whom the planet was named.

Although the stargazers of long ago didn't know it, they'd picked an especially suitable name for the planet. Jupiter is actually the largest planet in the *solar system.* The solar system consists of the sun and the nine planets, moons, and other objects that *orbit* it.

Jupiter as seen by a spacecraft.
A star background has been
added by an artist.

It may be difficult to imagine a planet of Jupiter's size. The diameter of Jupiter at its equator is 88,700 miles (142,800 km). This is over eleven times Earth's width. If Jupiter were a hollow ball, more than 1,000 planets the size of Earth could easily fit inside it. If you merged all the other planets in the solar system into one great big ball, Jupiter would still be larger.

Of the nine planets in the solar system, Jupiter is the fifth farthest from the sun. It's about 483½ million miles (778 million km) away from this fiery ball of heat and light. Earth is the third planet from the sun, only about 93 million miles (150 million km) away from it.

Like the other planets, Jupiter revolves around the sun. However, Jupiter is so far away from the sun that it takes the planet nearly twelve years (Earth time) to complete its orbit. Because Earth is so much closer to the sun, its orbit takes only 365 days or one year.

At the same time Jupiter orbits the sun, it also turns on its *axis*—an imaginary line through its center. All planets spin or rotate as they complete their paths around the sun. Jupiter spins more rapidly than any other planet. It rotates once every 9 hours and 55 minutes. The Earth rotates every twenty-four hours (one day).

THE FLUID PLANET

CHAPTER TWO

You could not walk on Jupiter. This is because Jupiter is not a solid planet the way Earth is. It is mostly a huge whirling ball of gases and liquids. Scientists think the planet may only have a small hardened core of rocky matter. That's why astronomers sometimes refer to Jupiter as the fluid planet.

The only portion of Jupiter that may be seen from Earth is the planet's outer *atmosphere.* Therefore, what we know about Jupiter is somewhat limited. However, if you looked at Jupiter through a telescope from Earth, you'd see a number of different markings on the planet's clouds. A series of dark stripes appear to encircle the planet. The size (width) and position of these dark regions change somewhat with the passage of time.

Between the dark belts on Jupiter, lighter zones appear. At times, the light areas may contain colorful swirls of orange, rust, red, yellow, beige, and white clouds.

Jupiter's brilliantly colored clouds are in constant motion. As the fastest spinning planet in the solar system, Jupiter's own rotational movement causes forceful winds. The winds push the clouds into their wildly colorful and ever-changing stripe, or belt, patterns.

At times, Jupiter's light zones may appear to be higher than the darker belts. Some scientists

This color-enhanced view of Jupiter exaggerates the color differences within the planet's naturally colorful atmosphere. The process is done to show detail more clearly within the clouds.

think this is because the light areas contain warmer gases. The warmer gases tend to rise quickly. There's less activity in the darker areas.

However, sometimes small light patches may be seen within the darker belts. The photographs returned to Earth from space *probes* show that these light blotches may actually be storm occurrences on Jupiter's clouds. In such instances, huge masses of rapidly swirling gases create serious atmospheric disturbances. The effect is very much like a hurricane on Earth.

These whirling gas pockets may be immense. Some are even larger than the planet Earth. A storm on Earth may continue for a matter of hours or perhaps days. But a storm on Jupiter may go on for hundreds of years.

One of the best known storm centers on Jupiter is called the Great Red Spot. It was first noticed by astronomers over three hundred years ago. The Great Red Spot looks like a large oval patch on Jupiter's clouds. The spot is 25,000 miles (40,250 km) long. This means that this storm area occupies a space on Jupiter that's three times the width of Earth! As the years pass, the Great Red Spot gradually shifts its position on the gaseous planet.

The composition of Jupiter's atmosphere differs vastly from that of Earth. Earth's atmosphere

A look at the
giant planet's
cloud tops. The
picture's most
striking feature is
the Great Red Spot.
This storm center is
large enough to
swallow up three Earths.

is largely made up of oxygen and nitrogen. But Jupiter's atmosphere is mostly hydrogen (84 percent) and helium (15 percent). The remaining one percent includes small amounts of other gases such as acetylene, ammonia, ethane, methane, carbon monoxide, phosphine, and water vapor.

The gases of Jupiter's atmosphere are not visible. Yet we can see the marvelously colored swirls of clouds within the planet's different belts and zones. This is because some of the varied materials that make up Jupiter's world have frozen and formed crystals. So we are actually looking at the crystallized form of the gases.

The clouds of Jupiter are so thick that we can't actually see Jupiter's surface. Jupiter's "surface" (the area beneath its clouds) is not a hardened

Jupiter's cloud tops in the planet's southern hemisphere are shown here. The white ovals are rising cloud columns. The largest of these ovals has a diameter about half that of Earth.

ONE MODEL OF JOVIAN INTERIOR

INTERNAL ENERGY SOURCE GRAVITATIONAL OR RADIOACTIVE

CLOUD TOPS

METALLIC HYDROGEN

ROCKY SILICATES/ METALLIC ELEMENTS

LIQUID AND/OR SOLID HYDROGEN

UPPER ATMOSPHERE
- WATER VAPOR AND WATER DROPLETS
- ICE CRYSTALS
- AMMONIA VAPOR
- AMMONIA DROPLETS
- AMMONIA CRYSTALS

(Left) A close-up of one of Jupiter's white ovals. Notice the dark rings around the edges of these rising cloud columns. The dark portions are regions of downward motion within the surrounding clouds. (Above) A model of Jupiter's interior shows the planet's various layers from its upper atmosphere to its inner rocky core.

solid, though, in the same way we think of a surface on Earth. Instead, Jupiter's surface is largely made up of hydrogen gas.

Scientists are not certain, but they suspect that there might be a deeper interior of liquid hydrogen that blankets the planet. They also think the innermost core of the planet—many thousands of miles beneath the clouds—may be made up of iron-bearing rocks.

The temperatures on Jupiter vary greatly on different levels of this fluid planet. Temperatures at the very top of Jupiter's cloud-filled atmosphere are extremely cold. It is difficult to imagine a colder environment. The average temperature is this area of the planet is approximately −200°F (−120°C).

The large brown oval photographed here by *Voyager 1* is actually an opening in Jupiter's upper clouds. When viewed from a higher point, it can provide information about deeper, warmer cloud levels.

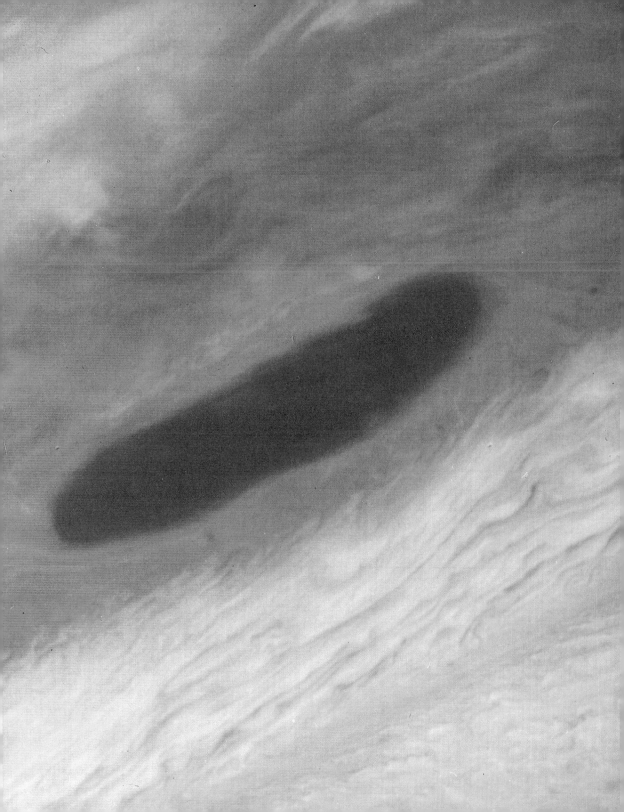

Under the clouds, Jupiter's atmosphere is considerably warmer. At this time, the temperature of Jupiter's surface is still unknown. However, it is believed that the planet's interior may be exceedingly hot.

In fact, the further you go toward the planet's center, the warmer the planet becomes.

Jupiter throws off practically double the energy it is given by the sun. This powerful energy source actually comes from Jupiter's own internal heat. The very center of this huge planet may reach a temperature of approximately 43,000°F (24,000°C).

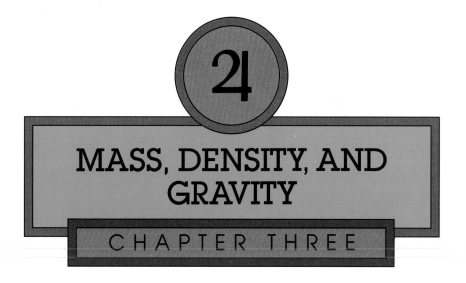

MASS, DENSITY, AND GRAVITY

CHAPTER THREE

Often in describing how the various planets are alike or different, astronomers will speak of a planet's *mass*. This term represents the planet's composition, or the total amount of material the planet is made up of. Jupiter has a considerably greater mass than Earth. It contains three hundred and eighteen times more material. In fact, Jupiter has the greatest mass of any planet in the solar system.

Density is another measure by which planets are often compared. The density of a planet tells us how compact or tightly fit together are the materials of which it is made. Although Jupiter is the largest planet, it has a low density. In fact, it is only about a quarter as dense as Earth. Earth has the highest density of any planet in the solar system.

Gravity is an unseen force that pulls objects toward the center of a planet. For example, if you toss a coin into the air, it will fall to the floor. Gravity pulls it back down. Gravity is what forces a kite to the ground once the wind no longer blows it through the air.

This gravitational pull operates on Jupiter and the other planets as well as on Earth. Jupiter has an extremely strong gravitational pull.

4

JUPITER'S MOONS AND RING

CHAPTER FOUR

Since the early 1970s, a series of space probes have been launched to help scientists learn more about Jupiter. By 1973, *Pioneer X*, an unmanned space probe, flew within about 81,000 miles (130,400 km) of the planet. *Pioneer X* provided valuable data about Jupiter's atmosphere as well as other important information.

In 1974, *Pioneer-Saturn*, another unmanned space probe, flew even closer to Jupiter. Passing within 26,000 miles (41,800 km) of the planet, it obtained close-up photographs of Jupiter's surface and supplied scientists with more detailed facts than they had ever had. Next, in March 1979, the U.S. *Voyager 1* probe approached Jupiter. *Voyager 1* enabled scientists to learn that Jupiter was

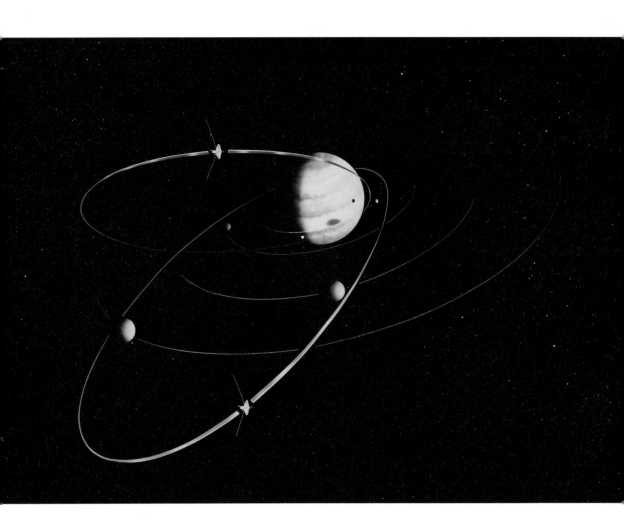

A painting of a space probe orbiting
Jupiter and its moons. The real
probe gathered information about
Jupiter's colors, its unusual features,
and the continual motion
within its atmosphere.

encircled by a ring. Later that year, (July 1979) the *Voyager 2* space probe took detailed photographs of Jupiter's four closest moons.

JUPITER'S MOONS

At present we know that Jupiter has sixteen known *satellites,* or moons. Some scientists think that there may be others as well. In 1610, Jupiter's largest four moons were discovered by a notable scientist and astronomer named Galileo. That's why they are called the Galilean satellites. These moons have been named Io, Europa, Ganymede, and Callisto and are bright enough to be visible with binoculars to the left and right of the planet.

Io

Io is the satellite or moon that most closely orbits Jupiter. According to ancient Greek myth, Io was a beautiful young girl. The all-powerful god Zeus (the Greek equivalent of the Roman's Jupiter) had fallen in love with her. But his wife was aware of Zeus's affection for the girl and became extremely jealous. To protect Io from his wife, Zeus turned the girl into a small cow. Her name was given to one of Jupiter's moons.

In some ways, Io is a unique moon. A photograph taken by *Voyager 1* had revealed a

Galileo at work. The discovery
of Jupiter's four closest
moons was among Galileo's
many achievements. Even as a
child, he'd shown a keen
interest in science and
frequently built his own toys.

An artist's illustration of
Jupiter and its four
Galilean satellites against
a starry background.

tentlike formation on Io's surface. By studying the photograph and the information gathered by *Voyager,* scientists made a fantastic discovery. They had unknowingly taken a picture of an erupting volcano. At the time *Voyager 1* photographed the volcano, it had been shooting its debris into space.

The news stirred the scientific community. In the past, the Earth had been the only place in the solar system where active volcanoes had been known to exist. Now Io was thought of as an active and exciting sphere.

Having discovered the first volcano, the researchers looked for others. They located a number of them, some of which were still erupting at the time they were photographed.

Earth's moon has numerous craters on its surface. These holes are believed to have been made by *asteroids, meteors,* and other bodies striking the moon early in its history. It is generally thought, therefore, that extensive craters are an indication of age. Io does not appear to have craters. Therefore, some scientists suggest that it may be the youngest body in the solar system.

Io's surface is covered by both dark and light spots, and a fantastic patchwork of colors caused by sulfur deposits: red, orange, yellow, white, and

In this painting, a *Voyager* spacecraft aims its instrument-scan platform directly at Jupiter.

Io, as photographed by
Voyager 1, from a distance
of 304,000 miles (489,440 km).
Notice the volcanic
explosion taking place
in the background.

A photo of Io clearly
showing the moon's
irregular depressions.

more. Scientists think that the spots may be the locations of both active and sleeping volcanoes.

Europa

Europa is Jupiter's second-closest moon. In Greek myth, Europa was another young and beautiful girl whom Zeus loved. Zeus had approached Europa in the form of a bull. The girl climbed on his back and together they flew off to a beautiful Greek island.

Europa is smaller than the Earth's moon. Unlike Io, it has no volcanoes or even high mountains.

Europa's surface is coated with ice. This blanket of frozen water is believed to be as thick as 60 miles or more (97 km) in some areas. Photographs taken by space probes show there are also dark lines across this moon's surface. These streaks may be cracks caused by heating, cooling, and the motion of the icy coating. Some scientists think that Europa's surface may be very much like the frozen Arctic zones on Earth.

Although Europa's surface is icy and cold, the young moon's interior is actually hot. Scientists are not sure why. They suspect that Europa's inner heat may result from the gravitational pull of other satellites as well as that of the planet Jupiter.

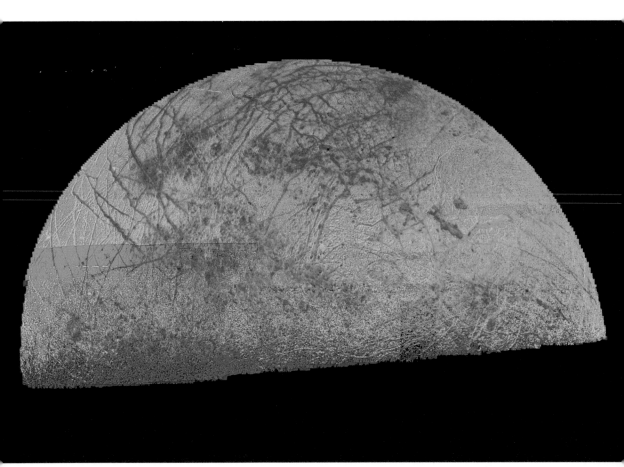

Here Europa is shown
through a false-color photo
combination. The red veinlike
features are believed
to be cracks in the
frozen water crust.

A view of Europa taken from a distance of 1.6 million miles (2.1 million km). Notice the scattered dark and bright regions on the moon's surface.

The heat and pressure from within may cause geysers of water to erupt on Europa. The cold outer temperatures cause this water to freeze immediately. Then it falls on Europa's surface as hail.

Ganymede

Ganymede is the third closest moon to Jupiter. Although all of Jupiter's Galilean moons are named after characters in Greek myths, Ganymede is the only one named for a male. Ganymede was a young boy who was carried away by Zeus to the home of the gods, where he became a cup-bearer who brought the gods their goblets of wine.

Ganymede is the largest of all of Jupiter's moons, nearly twice the size of the Earth's moon. Since Ganymede is covered with craters, scientists think that its surface must be very old.

About half of the satellite is water. Much of the water has frozen into ice. The light whitish areas seen on Ganymede are largely icy patches. There is also a large round dark region on this moon. Other dark areas exist on Ganymede as well; they contain dust, rock, and soil.

Ganymede's surface isn't smooth. Photographs show ridges, grooves, valleys, and regions that look as though they've been twisted. There are long slender ridges on Ganymede composed of ice, dust, and debris. These ridges may have formed from cracks in Ganymede's crust. Dark indentations or valleys are found between the moon's ridges.

Callisto

Callisto is the Galilean satellite or moon that is farthest from Jupiter. In Greek myth, Callisto was an unusually beautiful young girl who'd captured Zeus's attention. When his wife learned of Zeus's passion for the girl, she turned Callisto into a bear to make the youthful beauty unattractive to her husband. Zeus now feared for his young love's safety. To protect Callisto from hunters, he lifted her up to the heavens. There the girl sparkled among the stars as the Great Bear—whose brightest stars form the Big Dipper.

In some ways, Callisto is very much like its neighboring satellite Ganymede. This moon is heavily covered with craters, as revealed by photographs taken by the *Voyager* probes. Its rocky surface also is largely covered with ice.

The remaining twelve known satellites of Jupiter are not as large as the Galilean moons. Their diameters range from under 10 miles (16 km) for

This picture of Callisto, the outermost Galilean satellite, was taken by *Voyager 1* from a distance of about 5 million miles (8 million km).

A close-up of Callisto
showing its mixture of
ice and rock. Callisto's
upper surface is sometimes
called "dirty ice."

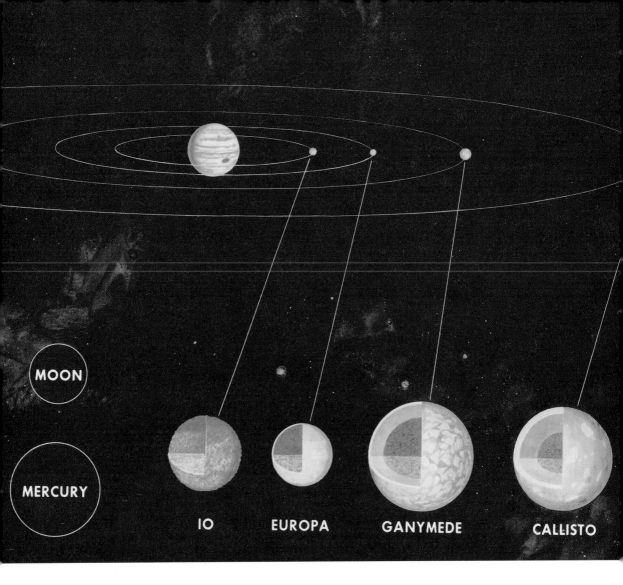

MOON

MERCURY

IO   EUROPA   GANYMEDE   CALLISTO

This cutaway drawing of
Jupiter's four inner moons
compares their large size
with that of Earth's moon
and the planet Mercury.

the smallest to over 100 miles (161 km) for the largest. These satellites were mostly found since the last century with powerful telescopes. The last few were discovered by the recent space probes.

JUPITER'S RING

Scientists have also discovered a faint slender ring around Jupiter. It is probably largely composed of dust particles. Only three other planets in the solar system have been shown to have rings. They are Saturn, Neptune, and Uranus.

THE FUTURE

CHAPTER FIVE

The exploration of any space frontier always brings up the question of whether life could exist elsewhere in the universe. We are almost certain that life, as we experience it on Earth today, could not survive on the frozen gaseous planet of Jupiter. At best, only robot explorers could ever spend time there.

Scientists expect to learn more about Jupiter within years to come. In October 1989, the *Galileo* mission to Jupiter was launched. This space probe was originally scheduled to leave Earth in 1982, but there were obstacles to overcome.

At first, completion of the shuttle's development was delayed. Then the launch was further postponed after the space shuttle *Challenger* exploded in January 1986, killing all the astronauts aboard.

Following the tragic *Challenger* disaster, stricter safety rules for all space probes were established. This meant that *Galileo* would have to be at least partially redesigned. The new rules prevented the *Galileo* from having a large liquid-fueled booster on board. The booster would have given the shuttle sufficient power to shoot directly to Jupiter.

Now engineers were faced with a challenging dilemma. They had to find an energy-efficient path that would allow the *Galileo* to reach and orbit Jupiter. To do this, they would have to make use of the gravitational pull of the other planets.

An oil portrait of Christa McAuliffe entitled *First Teacher in Space*. Ms. McAuliffe, a public school teacher chosen to go on this mission, died along with the other crew members when the *Challenger* exploded shortly after being launched.

Sharon Christa McAuliffe
First teacher in space.

This watercolor painting
entitled *Galileo Watches*
shows the ancient astronomer
viewing the *Galileo*
spacecraft named for him.

The engineers designed an unusual orbit for their space probe.

Galileo's new round-about orbit is as follows: First, *Galileo* was launched from the space shuttle *Atlantis* in October 1989 into a broad orbit around the sun, aimed in the direction of Venus. *Galileo* swung around Venus in February 1990 to pick up speed. It was assisted in doing so by Venus's gravitational pull, which gave it a small "kick."

Galileo continued in its orbit around the sun, but headed back to Earth. It received its second gravitational boost in December 1990, when the spacecraft passed Earth.

Galileo then heads toward the asteroid belt—a grouping of many thousands of small planetlike bodies that largely orbit the sun between Mars and Jupiter—arriving there in October 1991. It then heads back toward Earth.

Next, *Galileo* will swing around Earth for the second time in December 1992. At this point, it will have gained enough speed and power to reach Jupiter. It is scheduled to do so in December 1995.

In 1995, as *Galileo* approaches Jupiter, the spacecraft will launch a rapidly spinning probe straight into the gaseous atmosphere of the large planet. The probe will travel at a speed of over

The Jet Propulsion Laboratory's Deep Space
Network (DSN) shown here communicates with
and tracks spacecraft traveling in deep space.
It is hoped that new information collected by
DSN will lead to future scientific gains.

100,000 miles (161,000 km) per hour. It should send new information back to Earth about the makeup and structure of Jupiter's atmosphere.

After the probe has been released, the major portion of the *Galileo* spacecraft will continue on its journey. Over the following two years, it is expected to complete ten orbits of Jupiter. On each of its trips, the spacecraft will closely pass one of the planet's four closest moons.

The venture to Jupiter has excited many astronomers. Some scientists believe that Jupiter holds the key to solving many puzzling mysteries about the Earth and other planets. This is because of Jupiter's composition. The planet has a tremendous gravitational pull. The force of its gravity stopped gaseous elements found there, such as hydrogen and helium, from escaping. As a result, some scientists suspect that Jupiter's present composition may be very much like that of the other planets when they originally formed. This means that today Jupiter is probably somewhat similar to the way Earth was 4.6 billion years ago.

Jupiter may offer scientists an unusual opportunity to study the early history of the Earth and other planets. Learning more about Jupiter should yield better clues as to how the Earth actually evolved. Many scientific rewards will be gotten from future missions to Jupiter and other planets. Yet among the most exciting may be better understanding of our own planet's past.

FACT SHEET ON JUPITER

Symbol for Jupiter— ♃

Position—Jupiter is the fifth farthest planet from the sun. It is separated from Earth in the solar system by the planet Mars.

Rotation period—9 hours 55 minutes

Length of year—one year on Jupiter is just under twelve years' Earth time

Diameter—88,700 miles (142,800 kilometers)

Distance from the sun (depending on location in orbit)—least: 460,000,000 miles (740,000,000 kilometers); greatest: 507,000,000 miles (816,000,000 kilometers)

Distance from the Earth (depending on orbit)— least: 390,700,000 miles (628,760,000 kilometers); greatest: 600,000,000 miles (970,000,000 kilometers)

Number of known moons—16; the four closest moons to Jupiter were discovered by the astronomer Galileo in 1610. They are known as the Galilean moons.

GLOSSARY

Asteroid—any of thousands of small planet-like bodies that largely orbit the sun between Mars and Jupiter

Astronomers—scientists who study the location and movement of stars, planets, and other heavenly bodies

Atmosphere—the gaseous outer layer or "envelope" that surrounds a heavenly body

Axis—an imaginary line through the center of a planet

Density—the compactness of the materials that make up a planet

Gravity—the force that pulls objects toward the center of a planet

Mass—the body or bulk of a planet

Meteor—a small particle of matter in solar system

Orbit—the curved path followed by a body revolving around another body in space

Planet—any of nine large heavenly bodies that orbit the sun

Probe—a spacecraft carrying scientific instruments that orbits the sun on its way to one or more planets; in doing so, it may fly past a planet it has been aimed at, orbit the planet, or, in some cases, even land there. Planetary probes collect a great deal of data about a planet even from distances of millions or billions of miles

Satellite—a smaller body that orbits a planet

Solar system—the sun and the nine planets that orbit it, along with numerous smaller bodies such as asteroids, comets, and meteoric particles

FOR FURTHER READING

Asimov, Isaac. *Saturn: The Ringed Beauty.* Milwaukee, Wisconsin: Gareth Stevens, Inc., 1988.

Asimov, Isaac. *Uranus: The Topsy-Turvy Planet.* Milwaukee, Wisconsin: Gareth Stevens, Inc., 1987.

Baker, David. *Believe It or Not Space Facts.* Vero Beach, Florida: Rourke, 1987.

Branley, Franklin M. *The Planets in our Solar System,* rev. ed. New York: Crowell Junior Books, 1987.

Jay, Michael. *Planets.* New York: Franklin Watts, Inc., 1987.

Lampton, Christopher. *Stars and Planets: A Useful and Entertaining Tool to Guide Youngsters into the Twenty-first Century.* New York: Doubleday, 1988.

Rutherland, Johnathan. *The Planets.* New York: Random House, 1987.

Simon, Seymour. *Saturn.* New York: Morrow, 1985.

Simon Seymour. *Uranus.* New York: Morrow, 1987.

INDEX

ABOUT THE AUTHOR

Elaine Landau received her BA degree from New York University in English and Journalism and a master's degree in Library and Information Science from Pratt Institute in New York City.

Ms. Landau has worked as a newspaper reporter, an editor, and a youth services librarian. She has written many books and articles for young people. Ms. Landau lives in Sparta, New Jersey.